Comment Card

Books by Jim Daniels

Poetry

Places/Everyone
Punching Out
M-80
Niagara Falls
Blessing the House
Blue Jesus
Night with Drive-By Shooting Stars
Show and Tell
Street
Revolt of the Crash-Test Dummies
In Line for the Exterminator
From Milltown to Malltown
Having a Little Talk with Capital P Poetry
Birth Marks
Rowing Inland, Detroit
Street Calligraphy
The Middle Ages
Gun/Shy

Chapbooks

Factory Poems
On the Line
The Long Ball
Digger's Territory
Hacking It
Black Vinyl, Red Vinyl
Greatest Hits
Digger's Blues
Now Showing
All of the Above
Apology to the Moon
Human Engine at Dawn
Comment Card

Comment Card

Jim Daniels

The Cox Family Poetry Chapbook Series

Carnegie Mellon University Press
Pittsburgh 2024

Acknowledgments

Comment Card by Jim Daniels is the sixth volume in The Cox Family Poetry Chapbook Series of Carnegie Mellon University Press. The Press administrators and staff express their profound appreciation to Courtney, Lisa, and Jordan Cox for their generous support.

The author would like to acknowledge and thank the editors of the following magazines for first publishing these poems:

Cloudbank: "Thankful for the Moon"
Crazyhorse: "Dropping the Needles"
Hunger Mountain: "Snapper"
The Indianapolis Review: "Little God"
More in Time: A Tribute to Ted Kooser: "The Crucial Lack of Redemption"
Negative Capability: "Nostalgia for Three-Hole Punch"
The Paterson Literary Review: "Comment Card"
Pittsburgh Neighborhood Guidebook: "August Pause"
Plume: "Dinner at Lynn and Linda's with Ken and Jack"
SALT: "Unplugging the Machine," "Last Night in the Old House," "On the Waiting List"
Slipstream: "Death Watch," "The Lunar Module Stage of Life"
The Sun: "At 65"
The Windsor Review: "Migration"

Library of Congress Cataloging-in-Publication Data
. Names: Daniels, Jim, 1956- author.
Title: *Comment Card* / Jim Daniels.
Other titles: *Comment Card* (Compilation)
Description: Pittsburgh : Carnegie Mellon University Press, 2024. | Series: The Cox Family Poetry Chapbook series | Summary: "A poetry collection that hunts for meaning in the ordinary and astonishing. *Comment Card* offers up a world of juxtapositions, searching for equilibrium between the sublime and the mundane: a man watching young lovers kiss while poisoned ants rain down on his porch. A Christmas tree-needle collection and Jimmy Durante. The litter of a three-hole punch and a daughter leaving for college. Tamarinds and the International Space Station. A crushed snail and the Holy Trinity. These poems wonder, how did we get here, and, by the way, where are we?" —Provided by publisher.
Identifiers: LCCN 2023045645 | ISBN 9780887487019 (trade paperback)
Subjects: BISAC: POETRY / American / General | LCGFT: Poetry.
Classification: LCC PS3554.A5635 C66 2024 | DDC 811/.54--dc23/eng/20231010
LC record available at https://lccn.loc.gov/2023045645

Book design by Emily Stark & Connie Amoroso

10 9 8 7 6 5 4 3 2 1

Contents

Snapper

I'm addicted to the sound of trash
emptying on my laptop. Who threw
out the trash? Was it a rock?
Did it hit anyone? On dull days,

my 10th grade English teacher conducted
races in which we pushed a paper wad
across the floor with our noses. We enjoyed
it more than reading Shakespeare

though we missed Mr. K. spittling through
the air, reciting lines with vigor. He created
inappropriate nicknames for us.

A short man, he started with himself. He enjoyed
a pint or three down at the Friendly Sons
of St. Patrick Hall in the company of our fathers.

He gave us quizzes called Snappers that used
only half a sheet of paper. He was funny
about paper. I became a writer despite
my long nose and dusty knees.

You should have seen me push a paper ball
with that nose. Such authority. When I empty
my trash, I think of Shorty who knew
when we needed to get on our hands and knees

in the name of literature. Ah, the crackle of paper,
the empty trash can, the starting again,
back on the floor with no expectation
of prize or reward.

August Pause

to watch a young couple kiss in the street—
once, twice, pushing hard into each other
against a blue Kia with Ohio plates. Then
he slams the door. She stands on the curb
wobbling. He drives away slow. She's moving
into Next Door, Pittsburgh. I sit on my porch
watching dead ants fall from my roof
where the exterminator sprayed.
At the university where I teach, she'll get
oriented this week—that's the official plan.
What's their plan? Goodbye kisses
like that—young sugar kills an old man
like me, doubting their love can survive
the distance. Poison you can't see
or plan for. Raining ants out here.

Unplugging the Machine

*for my student who died of an aneurysm
while reading her poem aloud*

Last night, my loaded dream chambers splattered
imperfection and spite over the all-night walls
while my white-noise machine futilely hissed
out a polluted stream of nonsense prayers.

Yesterday in class while reading her poem
about nursing during the Korean War
one of my students lost her place forever.
We sat stunned, waiting for the last lines—

as if she might reemerge, find her place,
if only we sat long enough. Last night,
police slowly circled my block. Glass
loses to stone—someone had yearned

for that brief music. This morning I awoke
like a priest from the devil's dream.
Like a dog who'd paddled all night
through an ocean of dreamscape. My body

shook as I turned off the sleep machine.
But you want to know about the woman.
Today, they will unplug her, her twin sister
at her side pinching her nose against the burn—

memory's gunpowder, mercy's sting. Even here,
miles away, I cover my face, listen for silence.

On the Waiting List

Waiting for the moon to strike twelve
and find its other slipper. Waiting
for the shrinkage and settling
of the package. Waiting to squeeze
the air out. Waiting for the syringe.
The rush. Waiting for the trail
to end abruptly or empty out
onto a busy highway. Waiting
for the ambulance. Waiting
for someone to say *give*. Waiting
to punch out. Waiting for the lock
to lift the ship into deep water.
Waiting for the wind to cry Mary.
Waiting for the encore, the price check.
Waiting to get your money's worth.
To be another satisfied customer.
Waiting to accumulate.
Waiting for the next available
parking spot or bathroom stall.
Waiting through the previews.
Waiting for confirmation.
Waiting to recite the names
of the dead. Waiting for the echo.
Waiting for God, and in lieu of God,
waiting for the child, our child,
to emerge, bloody and screaming
after all the waiting.

Last Night in the Old House

wasn't all weepy like you might expect
given the money to change hands
atremble, given the capital letters
of the bank and the lowercase
of your heart, given the empty
drawers and the full boxes,
given the unplugged fridge
and the faint smell of ammonia,
given the strong smell of panic
and the weak taste of nerve
and the empty side
of the blow-up bed
and the unanswered questions
and the unfinished lists
and the stewing recriminations
and the thrown-away
keepsakes and the light-
headed lightening of the load
and the cloudy forecast
of the last time,
given the expansion of ghosts
and the inflated hiss
of air escaping
and the forwarded mail
and the reversed charges
and the paper
and the plastic
and the echo
of slammed doors
and the stench of disgust
and the rust and the dogged drip
of all the words spoken here

and broken here
and the red ink of a last kiss
and the red ink of future debt
and the blue light through
the window that you might
miss tomorrow,
given the unknown light to come,
given the known darkness descending,
given the hard bite of the key
in your clenched fist
so you won't lose it
before morning.

Thankful for the Moon

Last night I dreamt my teenage daughter clung
to me with the desperate love of childhood.
Snow today. While my teenage son
sleeps off his mother's tantrum, I shovel.

My daughter's half-empty cereal bowl
sticks to the counter. We're in the stone age—
she's helping archeologists who'd never find
the dishwasher. Ha, it's a winter blunderland.

Last night she retrieved the stale marshmallows
my wife had thrown out, then gorged herself.
I can't explain—use your imagination.
Last night I dreamt my mother could still see.

She was laughing at a comic strip. She'd clip
and send me corny ones. She can't even see
this sweet snow angling down like—
my imagination fails me. My daughter

mocked our grace prayer last night.
She does not believe in God, she said,
so why say what she's thankful for,
and to whom? *Us*, I should've said, *to us*.

I took away her dinner. We're not sure
about God ourselves, but look for something
positive in each day. That's corny. I'll take
corny. My wife made this great chili

with cornbread, but it was downhill
from there, a mudslide. Slogging through,

all of us covered in it. My son invented
a new face that made me want to smack him.

Too late to smack him, and I swore
I never would. He's bigger than me.
Raging accumulation in the just-cleared path
behind me. I'll have to re-shovel soon.

Or wake him up to help me.
I'm not up to that. He's not down with that.
I'm thankful I never hit him. About God,
I still wonder—as a child, I thought I knew.

Imagine someone inventing snow.
Be thankful, damn it. Yesterday,
while waiting to pick the kids up
from an after-school special

I watched the full moon. My car
idled in the parking lot. *Oh, moon,*
I said, and began to cry. My son
also thinks our grace is stupid.

Sometimes it takes me forever
to think of something to say.
In lieu of God, I have the moon.
Our moon, though there are many others.

Dropping the Needles

My daughter collected pine needles
in a thick, etched-glass box
with no obvious function.
The size of an ashtray with a lid—
designed to hold the souls of birds?

Every year till she was thirteen, she'd scoop
some needles into the box when we took
the tree down. Fifteen now. We keep the box
in the buffet with plastic flamingo coasters
and stained tablecloths left by the previous owner.

Jammed with pine, the box exploded into scent
when opened this year. No more room for needles.
Next year we might hand her a check in lieu
of artifice. Fake tree. What would Mrs. Bella's
tablecloths say? At fifteen, pine smell had turned me

nauseous. Drunk, I'd thrown up on my father's sleeping
bag, wiped it down, sprayed it with room freshener.
Has my daughter already thrown up on something of mine?
After we moved out, my father cut up the leaky tent
we'd slept in behind the house hot summer nights.

He used the pieces as tarps. I just might take up
smoking menthol cigarettes. The needle years
all mixed together. A lot of joy in that box, but not one
bird soul. Big trees, high ceilings, avid unwrappings
and hugs. Someday I'll tell her I turned our clocks back

an hour on Christmas Eve to steal a little sleep.
A little Santa secret. Maybe the year she remembers

to look for that box again. Those old linens, that big table
for the childless Bellas. The house weighted with mirrors
and portraits of each other. If I had their grandfather clock—

they wanted too much for it—I'd turn it back
a couple of years. Pine needles cannot get you high.
I never told my father about the sleeping bag.
He's 94. I loved swatting flies in that old tent.
They'd fill it up summer days when we aired it out.

I'd sweep their black punctuation into the ragged
essay of our weedy yard. I've got one of those tarps.
Just a whiff of it is enough. I want to collect
something as small and potent as pine needles.
Life is dangerous, and Christmas oddly depressing.

I sweep the trail of needles out the door
like Jimmy Durante sweeping up the spotlight
on his old TV show—yes, that sentimental.
I regret the year we'll only give her a check
folded in a Santa card.

Oh, but we'll have wrapping paper for years
to come. Maybe three or four. She didn't
leave Santa a note this year, a ritual her
and her brother kept too long. Mrs. Succotash,
where are you now? That can't be right.

Mrs. *Calabash*. Does she even know
who Jimmy Durante is? He made the most
of his big nose. My nose now loves the smell

of pine, despite dry needles like straight pins
with attitude, and the longing for old canvas.

I have not amused my children in years.
Embarrassment is dangerous, and Christmas
oddly menacing. We snatched our tree off a lot
this year. Five minutes. Zip, zoop, it's up.

I'd better stop before my hands get all sappy
or maybe it's too late. I may as well
just say it: my daughter's soul is in that box.

Nostalgia for Three-Hole Punch

My daughter the list keeper—
neat, deliberate cursive of casual
formality, civilized discussion.

For years, she punched holes in lined
paper for her series of color-coded
three-ring binders with a satisfying

whump. White circles littered the floors.
Don't ask why loose leaf did not serve.
She had a system. When she left for college

I licked my finger to lift them all up
from floors throughout the house.
The sad confetti of her leaving
in lieu of tears. The crooked shaky steps

of a stack of emptied binders.
The long packing list Scotch-taped
to her bedroom wall, everything crossed out.
I pulled it down, removed the tape.

I looked for the punch,
but she took it. We did not have
a civilized discussion before she left.
She hated spiral notebooks, the ragged fray

of torn sheets, the distorted circles
of cheap bent wire. Tears did not occur.
The hard thunk of the punch. Books always
get it wrong. Periods instead of commas.

Commas instead of periods.
Were they the crumbs of abandonment?
Maybe she will someday return—
she trailed ellipses out the door.

Migration

Jack Miner's Bird Sanctuary, Point Pelee, Canada

My father took me to Jack Miner's
to watch the Canada geese migrating
on the Sunday afternoon of one
of my first hangovers, right before
I stopped going anywhere with my father.

Thousands of geese filled the fields.
Fall leaves dropped off trees. Geese rose
and fell in honking waves of grace. It hurt
to watch them. I could still taste the mix
of liquors on my guilty breath. I started
tearing up against that wild wind
and turned away from him to scan the sky.

Fourteen. The hangover sharpened the view
and forced a squint. I guzzled a Coke
bottle plucked from a rusty old machine
and it bit into my gut. The geese knew
where they were going. My shoulders shook
with a heaving bout of tears I hadn't had
in years, my eyes so red I couldn't pretend.
They're beautiful I said, to say something.

*

When I was ten, my father and I dipped
for smelt at Point Pelee late at night
during the annual run, pulling in
a garbage can full. I waded cold water
and pulled the net toward shore
where he held the other end. Fires
in trash cans, drunk men cursing

into a clear night full of forgiving stars.
In the back of the car on the long ride home,
I pressed my ear against a rough plaid blanket
kept in the trunk for emergencies.

*

My father, retired from Ford's, writes
to tell me he saw the monarchs gather
at Point Pelee on their migration
to cross Lake Erie to Ohio.

Trying to catch butterflies
with my hands, I killed a few.
Monarchs, the only kind we saw
in fields between factories.
I could not name any of the pale
moths dying against the porch light
as I waited for my father
to come home from work.

*

Butterflies have short lives.
Geese stick together, mate for life.
Our migrations follow no pattern.
As I read his ragged scrawl,
I almost hear his voice, squawking
like wild geese, flapping across the page.

How do the monarchs know when to cross
the wide water? My instinct is to call it
love. Here at the end, I have to say
something.

The Crucial Lack of Redemption

I quit drinking when it turned into a part-time job.
    —Ted Kooser

I studied Spanish for years and years
but never learned to roll my R's. Like an engine
not turning over, slowly wearing the battery
down. This, after it took me eight years
of remedial speech to correct the slurring
of my words. This, before I began to drink
myself into slurring again. Though even
drunk I could not roll, could not flutter
those beautiful syllables. My father
never learned to say I love you
or use a computer or GPS. I've wasted
great quantities of unspared change
considering what is willful and what
cannot be helped and what
cannot be blamed. Lift the hood
and peer under as if something
could be done. Sometimes you just
have to slam that hood back down
and walk away. I'm a pretty good
walker, I've learned, wearing out
shoes and blues on city sidewalks
rubbing shoulders against brick for luck.
If I tell you I stopped drinking, that might
suggest a certain redemption, but there's
always that matter of the R's circling
like flocks of black birds in December
that I can never name.

Comment Card

Below zero—the hotel lost power—
frozen lines, broken sprinklers,
just when we had flicked our lights off
to slog our way toward sleep. Alarms
blazed their grim fiery order: *evacuate.*
The laminated Emergency Plan instructed
us to gather in the parking lot and wait.
Half-dressed, half-awake, we bristled
at the dark betrayal. A gaunt guy
in sweats and shorts jogged in place
exiled from the workout room
turning zombie blue.

Someone aimed a flashlight at our frozen feet
till the cleaning lady invited us to squeeze
into her tiny car, then started it up. Shoulders
rubbed. We did not sing songs. We shared
scraps and fragments of what brought us
to our lonely rooms. Bianca from house-
keeping shared cookies she'd stolen
for her two kids. Her English: *Take.*

None of us were meeting-cute.
No coincidental links or sitcom jokes.
The situation: I sat wedged between
an old businessman and a young saleswoman.
Bianca's old car smelled of Jesus air freshener.
Good heater, I said, and everyone agreed.
Our bodies, forced together,
grudged up extra heat.

The lights came on—you know that.
We fled the car in a mad frigid flurry.
The hotel offered us coffee and tea
in the lobby while we waited
for the all clear. We spread out over
stuffed couches. Bianca served us.
The manager chatted us up.
What can you do, he asked,
in weather like this?

Deathwatch

Rain thuds hollow against window glass,
fills gutters, puddles above sewer drains—
rain into sleet into mad bouncing dice
unlucky under streetlights.

Shame is a hard shovel against concrete,
edges curled from days humping coal
into the furnace before the transition
to gas. My mother transitions

into spirit in the next room. Water dripped
into her mouth with a syringe, sentences
drizzling slowly out, unfinished
into silence. About that shame—

to shovel through ice, toss it aside.
To bury her now, now, now.
Who is ashamed of what?
When do we quit calling survival

luck and start polishing our watch
faces? I am ashamed for wishing her
dead. All that rain out there—
evaporation invisible as faith in here.

Dinner at Lynn and Linda's with Ken and Jack

*Watch the International Space Station pass overhead from
several thousand worldwide locations. It is the third brightest
object in the sky and easy to spot if you know when to look up.*

Dinner tonight with two married gay couples
and their kids. The women have a boy.
The men have a girl. Off playing
video games in the basement.

*

Growing up in Detroit, our imaginations
limited by polluted night sky, oblivious
to constellations of shame, we teased
each other for admiring the moon.
I never looked both ways
before I crossed the street.

*

Linda looks it up on her phone.
Lynn rolls her eyes. Still, we step out
onto the porch at 8:17 in Pittsburgh,
on October 23, and wait. We have not
turned our furnaces on, any of us,
but we will soon. Couples lean
into each other for balance
on this dizzy planet.

*

Linda serves tamarinds. None of us
have tried them before. For dessert,
we eat donuts decorated with dulled

vampire teeth and blurry witches—
who can make anything graceful

on a donut? They're made to be gripped
with certainty and bit into and swallowed.
We discuss donuts and memories
of donuts and Halloween and costumes
we will no longer wear forever.

*

The kids stay inside. No interest
in seeing bright light zipper silent
across the sky, but the rest of us wait,
as we have waited for many things.
Porch light off, so as not to interfere,
yet tonight, we have found our way home.

*

After it passes, we go back in
to round up the kids, deal with life
on earth. The girl asleep in a father's arms,
the boy on the safe couch of home's dreamland.

*

Outside, we said nothing,
then we said *wow*—even that
too much in that grand silence
of changing seasons. Does the crew
circling the earth ever tire of wonder?

Ken's from Michigan, like me
with the flat vowels. Jack
was my student thirty years ago,
engaged to marry a girl.

Linda, my wife's oldest
and best friend. Linda and Lynn.
The Linns. What made her think
to watch the Space Station pass?

A white dot moving across the sky,
not a falling star, or a star at all.
I guess the kids take it for granted
what we can do now, the sky seamless,
not falling.

Little God

I've had enough of the Big God—
capital letters and Roman numerals
and the white flowing mane
and the brown flowing mane
and the crazy holy bird bouncing off
its reflection in the window.

Enormous erections of churches
and candles! All the burning!
Incense! Incensed! Purple cloth
and whispered recitation of sins
and the sad drizzle of the organ
and the sad collecting of money.

In the darkness tonight, I crushed
a snail under my shoe, perhaps
killing a little god. But that's the beauty
of little gods. I can't wait to find
a new one tomorrow!

The Lunar Module Stage of Life

starts around fifty
    and ends when you die
it involves lightheaded claustrophobia
    and memory-loss mattresses

a lack of home cooking
    and the betrayal of ancient color photos.
it starts when you lose your glasses
    and ends with political tunnel vision

it involves long goodbyes
    then short goodbyes
dreams of melted crayons
    and the smell of Play-Doh

an emphasis on plumbing
    not birth control
it involves a new twist on fate
    and a return to sacraments

sincere wishing at wishing wells
    and comparing notes on backs, knees,
and the parts that used to be naughty,
    but still failing the eye test, any test

it involves hair or lack thereof,
    pill counting and more pillows,
sleep or the lack thereof
    and hiring a house painter

jiggling the handle
    and lowering your standards

estimating your pre-adolescent
         and post-retirement income

imaginary demolition derbies
         and fender gender benders
it involves random blame
         and inspirational messages

fewer photographs
         more peeing
it involves the whitewashing
         of sex and the black funeral suit

obituaries not comics
         lists not paragraphs
the opposite of zero gravity
         and caving in on yourself

it involves defying
         in lieu of stiffening
faith in splashdown
         in lieu of drowning

it involves staring at the moon
         and the moon staring back
and the silent light
         and the light silence.

At 65

This morning I fell back
        into deep snow
and dug myself into an angel.

Yeah. I didn't tell anyone. I mean,
        c'mon, right?
Who did I think I was

kidding? I woke up then, as if touched
        by, not God, or iced fever,
but—some lost tender spirit?

What I want to say is that
        when I stood, I suddenly
lost all grace and nearly

fell onto my angel. My hand-
        print to save myself
lies where my heart is/was/

should be, a badge of snow
        in the dusted grass.
I noticed then the size

of my wings, their broad
        graceful arc—
who made those? I asked

as snow continued falling.
        I looked up into it,
almost dazzled again

        at 65.

Books in the Cox Family Poetry Chapbook Series